Author: Dan Meredith | Design and Production: Sophie Jewry
First Published in the UK by ReThink Press

ISBN: 978-1-78133-220-7

Legal Notices

A MESSAGE FROM DAN

I am someone who, until 2013, struggled to 'get shit done'.

Every deadline was met with a rush of panic to complete in time. There was a mountain of stress. I was continually forgetting important things, both business and personal.

In a nutshell, although I did (somehow) achieve some of my goals, I always felt that there had to be a better way - fortunately - I found that there was!

Back when I was a personal trainer, I had a very successful client called Keith. He showed me a very simple system that I have since (through trying a stupid amount of products, planners and programmes), refined into what is in your hands now.

Honestly, writing my book 'How To Be F*cking Awesome was a BREEZE compared to getting this 'just right'!

I told you I have spent a small fortune on planners, and found the complexity of some of them was overwhelming for many:

...trying to break down goals to figure out how to hit targets you had no clue how to get to!

...getting confused at what you were supposed to put where, and then somehow remembering to review it/do 'stuff' at the right time!

...so many damn boxes to fill in that you end up making a mess of the thing (and I have a weird obsession with stationery – but that's for another time..) and have no idea what you were doing!

For someone who has a very busy brain, multiple areas of my life I want to work on, a variety of businesses to grow, people I need to connect with - as well as trying to stay fit, spend time with important people and, you know, have fun - I needed something a) effective and b) simple.

So, I 'Danified' it.

I have based this around the principles that have worked for me, thousands of clients, and pretty much anyone who gives it a go in a #ballsdeep kinda way. That principle is continuous improvement. As you will find out, the 'theme' of the planner is to take action, every day, with a simple system, and daily, weekly and monthly reviews to keep you on track.

(and FYI if you DO want something a little more 'advanced' I 100% recommend my friends at www.bestself.co)

But with me?

No big scary seemingly impossible goals.

No fiddly OTT guides to figure out what the hell you are doing.

Just a 'big idea', knowing truly where you are
- followed up by consistent daily action.

Simple, eh?

I truly hope you get a lot of value from this planner. I have been using this system for over two years as of writing, and I have gone from a simple plum from Somerset with all the debt from opening my gym…

…to multiple businesses across marketing, copywriting, coaching, supplements, fitness, tens of thousands of people across **Coffee With Dan** and **Espresso With Dan**… oh and a bestselling book.

Which is nice.

;-)

Anyways enough of my nonsense... now turn the page and crack the fuck on!

HOW TO USE THIS BOOK

This book is your book to do with as you see fit. You could be a complete fruitcake like me, keep it pristine, and write in between the lines…

Or you can doodle all over it, deface my face, put stickers in it and write wherever you bloody well please.

The choice, as always, is yours – but the most important thing is you actually USE IT!

It is based around 3 simple elements:

REVIEW | PLAN | DO

That really is it!

Honestly, if you follow the system you will be amazed how much shit you have got done and brilliantly how much shit you can get done…and how much shit you DON'T have to do.

Been revolutionary for me...

Good luck and have fun!

MONTH LIFE AUDIT AND REVIEW

How can you improve if you don't know where you're starting from? Well, you can't.

I have listed 8 areas that from the thousands of people I have coached came up over and over again. Please feel free to add in ANY areas you too would like to improve, that's what the blank lines are for.

They are: business, bank balance, network, career, friendships, relationships, fitness and rest and relaxation. What I want you to do is be brutally honest with yourself, and rate yourself from 1 to 10 (1 = shit, 10 = awesome)

What you get from this is 2 things; the first is a 'total score' - the goal (over time) is to get this score as high as you honestly can. The second to find your 3 lowest scores. Because those 3 low scores? Well that's the 'backbone' of what you are going to work on for the following 4 weeks.

The planning cycle I am going to outline repeats in 4 week phases, 3 times, to make a total of 12 weeks of Getting Sh*t Done.

The life audit review page is a chance to determine why you think those scores are low, and then write down any ideas you might have to improve them.

THE BIG 3

Once you've done your review, take the 3 areas that you are going to improve, and write them down in the 1-2-3 sections at the top. After that, you are going to come up with 3 action steps (aka things you can do) to improve them.

Please note, there are no right or wrong answers here. You have to be honest with yourself and figure out what you could genuinely do to improve those areas. Don't overthink this bit - just give yourself some realistic (but challenging!) steps you could take to improve.

At the end of this page is a little box, and here I want you to write a reward that you are going to give yourself if you smash your month. It's important to reward success and I'll show you how I do it in just a moment.

WEEKLY BRAINDUMP AND THE 3/5 SYSTEM

Now, I'm going to walk you through the 'meat' of this planner with the system that pretty much changed my life - the weekly Sunday braindump and 3/5 system.

For the braindump I prefer Sunday, as it clears your head for the week coming. Sit down, ideally with no distractions - I find music helps, and simply write out EVERYTHING you have to do.

Really - everything.

It doesn't matter whether it's business or personal or chores or admin, it all goes down here. Then, once you have got it all out of your head, you are going to rank your items.

You want to be mindful of your 3+3 goals when you do this but you rank each line from 1 to 3.

1 = **Takes you closer to your 3+3 goal**. Only you can do it. It's also business critical, time bound/urgent, potentially 'life changing' - in other words the important shit that actually matters!

2 = **Still important, but could perhaps be handled by someone else**, or isn't as time critical. Needs to be done, but is perhaps more important to someone else than you.

3 = **Not urgent** or time bound, would like to be done 'sometime' but if it doesn't happen isn't the end of the world.

Now, here's the kicker...

You are only going to give a shit about the '1s'.

What you are going to do is take all those '1s' and put a minimum of 3 and a maximum of 5 of them in your planner EVERY DAY in the 'Important stuff' section on your day planner.

Your daily goal is simply to complete a minimum of 3 important tasks, and a maximum of 5. The reason this has been such a game changer for me is it forces you to really focus on what's important. If you have too many 1s? You are either kidding yourself or doing far too much and likely won't achieve anything as you are TOO busy. If you don't have enough '1s' - you need to do more.

See how simple that is?

Now, IF you do all 5 from your 'important stuff' box; by all means go back to your weekly braindump and cross of a few '2's and '3's. Equally, you can do nothing - that's up to you.

If you miss 1 or 2 from your 'important stuff' list, don't beat yourself up - either roll it over to another day, or guess what... it wasn't 'that' important in the first place!

This system is completely self-auditing.

If you keep failing to complete your 3/5 important things every day, there is an underlying reason why you are not doing what you said you would do - you need to reflect on that...or as I would, get over yourself and do the bloody work!

If you are doing all 3/5 important things, plus loads of '2s' and '3s' then you aren't challenging yourself. You're either doing lots of 'busy work' to make yourself feel good OR you're ignoring your 3+3 OR your big idea/big why/what you want to achieve isn't big enough for you.

Clever, eh?

DAY PLANNERS

After the 3/5 part of this, fill in the rest of the day planner.

The sections are:

Get shit done - things you need to do that day (and 2's or 3's you want to do, life stuff, pay bills, pick up shopping etc) - write em down and strike em off!

Daily agenda - I always advise a 2-hour block every day where you focus on your most important work, plus any appointments/meetings/calls you need to have go here.

Daily review - out of 10, how good was your day? A little bit of self-reflection and a few notes on what went right/wrong. Reviewing yourself often is a really important part of growth. Do it before bed and clear your head!

The area marked "Notes" on the left-hand side is for any mad scribblings or, you know, notes - and I have also included a little motivational quote per day, because everyone loves a good quote don't they...

MONTHLY BIG GOAL REVIEW

Every 4 weeks you are going to do big goal review. As always scored from 1 to 10 (1= shit, 10= awesome).

Go back to your big 3. For each of them you listed 3 action steps. I want you to rate each of these steps for IMPLEMENTATION and RESULTS. Then, next to your score, jot down any notes on why you think you got the figure you did.

Again, you will get a total. This is my advice:

Your maximum score can be 180 (perfect 10 for implementation and results for all 3 BIG GOALS).

If you scored an average of 7 on everything you would get 126, and if you score 126 or more? Then you get to treat yourself to the reward you promised yourself at the start of the 4 weeks.

If you didn't, no cake for you and better luck next month! Or, if you are a bit of a sadist who likes to push themselves to do ridiculous things, feel free to up the score to whatever pushes you the most!

Like anything in life, if you want to achieve something it takes discipline - and if you do stick with this? You really can change your life, times infinity +1!

Finally, there is a box for you to review the month overall. This is helpful to refer back to when you are having a bad/less successful month to see what you did in a good month so you can copy that again.

Once you have done that? You turn the page and start over again…

12 WEEK REVIEW

Once you have fully gone through 1 cycle of my 'I GET SH*T DONE' planner, we review the 12 weeks.

You will have a few questions to answer. I'll ask you to highlight your wins and losses for the month too.

Self-review and reflection is key. Looking back over 12 weeks, if you have taken action, a lot will have changed. At this point you can either take a little break for a week or so, or you can #bemoredan and buy another planner… ;-)

FOLLOW THIS SYSTEM IT WORKS!
NOW IT'S TIME TO

WHY THE FUCK AM I DOING THIS?
WHO THE HELL AM I DOING THIS FOR?
WHAT DO I WANT MY LIFE TO LOOK LIKE IN 12 WEEKS?

Ok, we start off with the 'big ideas' and the 'big whys' of the next 12 weeks.

I have found that going BIG has been a huge motivator for me to change my life for the better. Where I struggled was how to break down 3-month (let alone 1- to 10-year) goals! into something I could actually focus on.

So, I narrowed it down to 3 big concepts:

Why the fuck am I doing this - state to yourself WHY you are going to make the changes you are going to make. Knowing where you are at the start is key to change

Who the hell am I doing this for - whether it's for yourself, a loved one, family or another reason; knowing WHO you are going to do this for helps keep you going.

What do I want my life to look like in 12 weeks - the point of this planner is that it can help you improve ANY area of your life. Whether it's business, personal, spiritual, fitness, fun - whatever - take stock of where you are now, and then write out what you want your life to look like in 12 weeks' time.

Visualisation is key, and knowing what you want your life to look like after committing to 12 weeks of ACTION is a huge motivator.

My advice?

If you can spare 30 seconds at the start/end of your day to re-read these, it will really help. At the very least, have a read over once a week to keep your mind on track.

Equally, when the going gets tough - and it will - come back to read these to remind you of the important reasons you committed to doing this in the first place.

WHY THE FUCK AM I DOING THIS?

WHO THE HELL AM I DOING THIS FOR?

WHAT DO I WANT MY LIFE TO LOOK LIKE IN 12 WEEKS?

MONTHLY LIFE AUDIT

	SCORE
BUSINESS	
BANK BALANCE	
NETWORK	
CAREER	
FRIENDSHIPS	
RELATIONSHIPS	
FITNESS	
REST AND RELAXATION	
TOTAL SCORE	

MONTHLY LIFE AUDIT REVIEW

THE BIG 3: MONTH AHEAD GOAL SETTING

GOAL: _____

1
    A: _____
    B: _____
    C: _____

GOAL: _____

2
    A: _____
    B: _____
    C: _____

GOAL: _____

3
    A: _____
    B: _____
    C: _____

MY 'GOT SHIT DONE' REWARD FOR SMASHING THIS MONTH

_____

_____

WEEK 1

WEEKLY BRAINDUMP

**IT ALL STARTS WITH ONE SMALL STEP IN THE RIGHT DIRECTION.
ALL YOU HAVE TO DO IS KEEP ON WALKING.**

#BeMoreDan

WEEKLY BRAINDUMP

RANK

MY 3 BIG GOALS REMINDER: WHAT AM I FOCUSING ON THIS MONTH?

1

2

3

NOTES

DAY: DATE:

IMPORTANT STUFF (3/5)	

5-6AM	
6-7AM	
7-8AM	
8-9AM	
9-10AM	
10-11AM	
11AM-12PM	
12-1PM	
1-2PM	
2-3PM	
3-4PM	
4-5PM	
5-6PM	
6-7PM	
7-8PM	
8-9PM	
9-10PM	
10-11PM	
11PM-12AM	

GET SHIT DONE

☐
☐
☐
☐
☐
☐
☐
☐
☐
☐
☐
☐

DAILY REVIEW   **SCORE:** [ ]

> "YOUR TASK IS TO STAND STRAIGHT;
> NOT TO BE HELD STRAIGHT."
> **MARCUS AURELIUS**

DAY: DATE:

IMPORTANT STUFF (3/5)

GET SHIT DONE

- [ ]
- [ ]
- [ ]
- [ ]
- [ ]
- [ ]
- [ ]
- [ ]
- [ ]
- [ ]
- [ ]

DAILY REVIEW   SCORE:

5-6AM	
6-7AM	
7-8AM	
8-9AM	
9-10AM	
10-11AM	
11AM-12PM	
12-1PM	
1-2PM	
2-3PM	
3-4PM	
4-5PM	
5-6PM	
6-7PM	
7-8PM	
8-9PM	
9-10PM	
10-11PM	
11PM-12AM	

"NEVER LET THE FUTURE DISTURB YOU. YOU WILL MEET IT, IF YOU HAVE TO, WITH THE SAME WEAPONS OF REASON WHICH TODAY ARM YOU AGAINST THE PRESENT."

NOTES

DAY: DATE:

IMPORTANT STUFF (3/5)

	5-6AM
	6-7AM
	7-8AM
	8-9AM
	9-10AM
	10-11AM
	11AM-12PM

GET SHIT DONE

	☐	12-1PM	
	☐	1-2PM	
	☐	2-3PM	
	☐	3-4PM	
	☐	4-5PM	
	☐	5-6PM	
	☐	6-7PM	
	☐	7-8PM	
	☐	8-9PM	
	☐	9-10PM	
	☐	10-11PM	

DAILY REVIEW   SCORE: ☐

11PM-12AM	

"LIVE FOR SOMETHING RATHER THAN DIE FOR NOTHING."
GEORGE PATTON

DAY: DATE:

IMPORTANT STUFF (3/5)		5-6AM	

	5-6AM	

IMPORTANT STUFF (3/5)

	5-6AM
	6-7AM
	7-8AM
	8-9AM
	9-10AM
	10-11AM

GET SHIT DONE

		11AM-12PM
	☐	12-1PM
	☐	1-2PM
	☐	2-3PM
	☐	3-4PM
	☐	4-5PM
	☐	5-6PM
	☐	6-7PM
	☐	7-8PM
	☐	8-9PM
	☐	9-10PM
	☐	10-11PM

DAILY REVIEW   **SCORE:** ☐

11PM-12AM	

"IT'S GOING TO BE HARD BUT HARD IS NOT IMPOSSIBLE"

NOTES

DAY: DATE:

IMPORTANT STUFF (3/5)		5-6AM	

IMPORTANT STUFF (3/5)

GET SHIT DONE	
	☐
	☐
	☐
	☐
	☐
	☐
	☐
	☐
	☐
	☐
	☐

DAILY REVIEW	SCORE:

5-6AM	
6-7AM	
7-8AM	
8-9AM	
9-10AM	
10-11AM	
11AM-12PM	
12-1PM	
1-2PM	
2-3PM	
3-4PM	
4-5PM	
5-6PM	
6-7PM	
7-8PM	
8-9PM	
9-10PM	
10-11PM	
11PM-12AM	

"NEARLY ALL MEN CAN STAND ADVERSITY, BUT IF YOU WANT TO TEST A MAN'S CHARACTER, GIVE HIM POWER."
ABRAHAM LINCOLN

NOTES

DAY: DATE:

IMPORTANT STUFF (3/5)		5-6AM	

	6-7AM	
	7-8AM	
	8-9AM	
	9-10AM	
	10-11AM	

GET SHIT DONE

	☐	11AM-12PM	
	☐	12-1PM	
	☐	1-2PM	
	☐	2-3PM	
	☐	3-4PM	
	☐	4-5PM	
	☐	5-6PM	
	☐	6-7PM	
	☐	7-8PM	
	☐	8-9PM	
	☐	9-10PM	
	☐	10-11PM	

DAILY REVIEW   SCORE: [   ]   11PM-12AM

"DON'T EVER MISTAKE MY SILENCE FOR IGNORANCE, MY CALMNESS FOR ACCEPTANCE OR MY KINDNESS FOR WEAKNESS. COMPASSION AND TOLERANCE ARE NOT A SIGN OF WEAKNESS, BUT A SIGN OF STRENGTH." DALAI LAMA

35

NOTES

DAY: DATE:

IMPORTANT STUFF (3/5)		5-6AM	

5-6AM	
6-7AM	
7-8AM	
8-9AM	
9-10AM	
10-11AM	
11AM-12PM	
12-1PM	
1-2PM	
2-3PM	
3-4PM	
4-5PM	
5-6PM	
6-7PM	
7-8PM	
8-9PM	
9-10PM	
10-11PM	
11PM-12AM	

IMPORTANT STUFF (3/5)

GET SHIT DONE

☐
☐
☐
☐
☐
☐
☐
☐
☐
☐
☐
☐
☐
☐

DAILY REVIEW   **SCORE:** [ ]

> "DON'T LIMIT YOUR CHALLENGES;
> CHALLENGE YOUR LIMITS."
> JERRY DUNN

WEEK 2

WEEKLY BRAINDUMP

THERE IS NO MAGIC PILL, INSTANT SUCCESS OR QUICK FIX. FOR ANY BUSINESS, SUCCESS TAKES CONSISTENT TIME, EFFORT AND COMMITMENT.

#BeMoreDan

WEEKLY BRAINDUMP

MY 3 BIG GOALS REMINDER: WHAT AM I FOCUSING ON THIS MONTH?

1

2

3

NOTES

DAY:

DATE:

IMPORTANT STUFF (3/5)

GET SHIT DONE

- [ ]
- [ ]
- [ ]
- [ ]
- [ ]
- [ ]
- [ ]
- [ ]
- [ ]
- [ ]
- [ ]
- [ ]

DAILY REVIEW   SCORE: [ ]

5-6AM	
6-7AM	
7-8AM	
8-9AM	
9-10AM	
10-11AM	
11AM-12PM	
12-1PM	
1-2PM	
2-3PM	
3-4PM	
4-5PM	
5-6PM	
6-7PM	
7-8PM	
8-9PM	
9-10PM	
10-11PM	
11PM-12AM	

"THE FIRST RULE IS TO KEEP AN UNTROUBLED SPIRIT. THE SECOND IS TO LOOK THINGS IN THE FACE AND KNOW THEM FOR WHAT THEY ARE."
MARCUS AURELIUS

NOTES

DAY: DATE:

IMPORTANT STUFF (3/5)		5-6AM	

IMPORTANT STUFF (3/5)

	5-6AM	
	6-7AM	
	7-8AM	
	8-9AM	
	9-10AM	
	10-11AM	

GET SHIT DONE

		11AM-12PM	
	☐	12-1PM	
	☐	1-2PM	
	☐	2-3PM	
	☐	3-4PM	
	☐	4-5PM	
	☐	5-6PM	
	☐	6-7PM	
	☐	7-8PM	
	☐	8-9PM	
	☐	9-10PM	
	☐	10-11PM	

DAILY REVIEW   SCORE: ☐

| | 11PM-12AM | |

"THOSE WHO ARE SKILLED IN COMBAT DO NOT BECOME ANGERED, THOSE WHO ARE SKILLED AT WINNING DO NOT BECOME AFRAID. THUS THE WISE WIN BEFORE THE FIGHT, WHILE THE IGNORANT FIGHT TO WIN."
SUN TZU

NOTES

DAY: DATE:

IMPORTANT STUFF (3/5)

GET SHIT DONE

- [ ]
- [ ]
- [ ]
- [ ]
- [ ]
- [ ]
- [ ]
- [ ]
- [ ]
- [ ]
- [ ]
- [ ]

DAILY REVIEW   SCORE:

5-6AM	
6-7AM	
7-8AM	
8-9AM	
9-10AM	
10-11AM	
11AM-12PM	
12-1PM	
1-2PM	
2-3PM	
3-4PM	
4-5PM	
5-6PM	
6-7PM	
7-8PM	
8-9PM	
9-10PM	
10-11PM	
11PM-12AM	

"DON'T EXPECT ANYONE TO GIVE YOU ANYTHING.
IF YOU REALLY BELIEVE IN SOMETHING,
THEN FIGHT FOR IT."
DAMON DASH

NOTES

DAY: DATE:

IMPORTANT STUFF (3/5)		5-6AM	

IMPORTANT STUFF (3/5)

GET SHIT DONE

	☐
	☐
	☐
	☐
	☐
	☐
	☐
	☐
	☐
	☐
	☐
	☐
	☐

DAILY REVIEW   SCORE: [   ]

5-6AM	
6-7AM	
7-8AM	
8-9AM	
9-10AM	
10-11AM	
11AM-12PM	
12-1PM	
1-2PM	
2-3PM	
3-4PM	
4-5PM	
5-6PM	
6-7PM	
7-8PM	
8-9PM	
9-10PM	
10-11PM	
11PM-12AM	

> "YOU HAVE POWER OVER YOUR MIND
> - NOT OUTSIDE EVENTS. REALISE THIS,
> AND YOU WILL FIND STRENGTH."
> MARCUS AURELIUS

49

NOTES

DAY: DATE:

IMPORTANT STUFF (3/5)

5-6AM	
6-7AM	
7-8AM	
8-9AM	
9-10AM	
10-11AM	
11AM-12PM	
12-1PM	
1-2PM	
2-3PM	
3-4PM	
4-5PM	
5-6PM	
6-7PM	
7-8PM	
8-9PM	
9-10PM	
10-11PM	
11PM-12AM	

GET SHIT DONE

- ☐
- ☐
- ☐
- ☐
- ☐
- ☐
- ☐
- ☐
- ☐
- ☐
- ☐
- ☐

DAILY REVIEW   SCORE: [   ]

"A LION SLEEPS IN THE HEART OF EVERY BRAVE MAN."
TURKISH PROVERB

DAY: DATE:

IMPORTANT STUFF (3/5)

5-6AM	
6-7AM	
7-8AM	
8-9AM	
9-10AM	
10-11AM	

GET SHIT DONE

11AM-12PM	
12-1PM	
1-2PM	
2-3PM	
3-4PM	
4-5PM	
5-6PM	
6-7PM	
7-8PM	
8-9PM	
9-10PM	
10-11PM	

DAILY REVIEW   SCORE:

11PM-12AM	

"BRAVERY IS THE CAPACITY TO PERFORM PROPERLY EVEN WHEN SCARED HALF TO DEATH."
OMAR

NOTES

DAY: DATE:

IMPORTANT STUFF (3/5)

5-6AM	
6-7AM	
7-8AM	
8-9AM	
9-10AM	
10-11AM	
11AM-12PM	
12-1PM	
1-2PM	
2-3PM	
3-4PM	
4-5PM	
5-6PM	
6-7PM	
7-8PM	
8-9PM	
9-10PM	
10-11PM	
11PM-12AM	

GET SHIT DONE

- [ ]
- [ ]
- [ ]
- [ ]
- [ ]
- [ ]
- [ ]
- [ ]
- [ ]
- [ ]
- [ ]
- [ ]

DAILY REVIEW   SCORE: [   ]

"OBSTACLES DON'T HAVE TO STOP YOU.
IF YOU RUN INTO A WALL, DON'T TURN AROUND
AND GIVE UP. FIGURE OUT HOW TO CLIMB IT,
GO THROUGH IT, OR WORK AROUND IT."
MICHAEL JORDAN

WEEK 3

WEEKLY BRAINDUMP

**STOP. GIVING. UP. START FOLLOWING UP.
BE A LITTLE CHEEKY. SEE WHAT HAPPENS.**

#BeMoreDan

WEEKLY BRAINDUMP

RANK

MY 3 BIG GOALS REMINDER: WHAT AM I FOCUSING ON THIS MONTH?

1

2

3

NOTES

DAY: **DATE:**

IMPORTANT STUFF (3/5)

5-6AM	
6-7AM	
7-8AM	
8-9AM	
9-10AM	
10-11AM	
11AM-12PM	
12-1PM	
1-2PM	
2-3PM	
3-4PM	
4-5PM	
5-6PM	
6-7PM	
7-8PM	
8-9PM	
9-10PM	
10-11PM	
11PM-12AM	

GET SHIT DONE

☐
☐
☐
☐
☐
☐
☐
☐
☐
☐
☐
☐

DAILY REVIEW   SCORE: ☐

"REMEMBER THIS. HOLD ON TO THIS. THIS IS THE
ONLY PERFECTION THERE IS, THE PERFECTION
OF HELPING OTHERS. THIS IS THE ONLY THING WE
CAN DO THAT HAS ANY LASTING MEANING.
THIS IS WHY WE'RE HERE."
ANDRE AGASSI

NOTES

DAY:

DATE:

IMPORTANT STUFF (3/5)

GET SHIT DONE

- [ ]
- [ ]
- [ ]
- [ ]
- [ ]
- [ ]
- [ ]
- [ ]
- [ ]
- [ ]
- [ ]
- [ ]

DAILY REVIEW   SCORE:

5-6AM	
6-7AM	
7-8AM	
8-9AM	
9-10AM	
10-11AM	
11AM-12PM	
12-1PM	
1-2PM	
2-3PM	
3-4PM	
4-5PM	
5-6PM	
6-7PM	
7-8PM	
8-9PM	
9-10PM	
10-11PM	
11PM-12AM	

"THERE ARE NO SECRETS TO SUCCESS.
IT IS THE RESULT OF PREPARATION, HARD WORK,
LEARNING FROM FAILURE."
COLIN POWELL

DAY: DATE:

IMPORTANT STUFF (3/5)

GET SHIT DONE

	☐
	☐
	☐
	☐
	☐
	☐
	☐
	☐
	☐
	☐
	☐
	☐

DAILY REVIEW   SCORE: [ ]

5-6AM	
6-7AM	
7-8AM	
8-9AM	
9-10AM	
10-11AM	
11AM-12PM	
12-1PM	
1-2PM	
2-3PM	
3-4PM	
4-5PM	
5-6PM	
6-7PM	
7-8PM	
8-9PM	
9-10PM	
10-11PM	
11PM-12AM	

"CHANGE IS THE LAW OF LIFE. AND THOSE WHO LOOK ONLY TO THE PAST OR PRESENT ARE CERTAIN TO MISS THE FUTURE."
JOHN F. KENNEDY

NOTES

DAY: DATE:

IMPORTANT STUFF (3/5)

....

GET SHIT DONE

☐
☐
☐
☐
☐
☐
☐
☐
☐
☐
☐
☐
☐

DAILY REVIEW   SCORE: ☐

5-6AM	
6-7AM	
7-8AM	
8-9AM	
9-10AM	
10-11AM	
11AM-12PM	
12-1PM	
1-2PM	
2-3PM	
3-4PM	
4-5PM	
5-6PM	
6-7PM	
7-8PM	
8-9PM	
9-10PM	
10-11PM	
11PM-12AM	

> "EVERYTHING WE HEAR IS AN OPINION,
> NOT A FACT. EVERYTHING WE SEE IS
> A PERSPECTIVE, NOT THE TRUTH."
> MARCUS AURELIUS

NOTES

DAY:

DATE:

IMPORTANT STUFF (3/5)

GET SHIT DONE

- [ ]
- [ ]
- [ ]
- [ ]
- [ ]
- [ ]
- [ ]
- [ ]
- [ ]
- [ ]
- [ ]
- [ ]
- [ ]

DAILY REVIEW   SCORE:

5-6AM	
6-7AM	
7-8AM	
8-9AM	
9-10AM	
10-11AM	
11AM-12PM	
12-1PM	
1-2PM	
2-3PM	
3-4PM	
4-5PM	
5-6PM	
6-7PM	
7-8PM	
8-9PM	
9-10PM	
10-11PM	
11PM-12AM	

"WARRIORS ARE NOT ALWAYS THE FASTEST OR STRONGEST MEN. STRENGTH AND SPEED CAN BE DEVELOPED THROUGH TRAINING."

NOTES

DAY: DATE:

IMPORTANT STUFF (3/5)		5-6AM	

IMPORTANT STUFF (3/5)

_____

_____

_____

. . . .

GET SHIT DONE

_____	☐
_____	☐
_____	☐
_____	☐
_____	☐
_____	☐
_____	☐
_____	☐
_____	☐
_____	☐
_____	☐
_____	☐

DAILY REVIEW   SCORE: [   ]

_____

_____

_____

_____

5-6AM	
6-7AM	
7-8AM	
8-9AM	
9-10AM	
10-11AM	
11AM-12PM	
12-1PM	
1-2PM	
2-3PM	
3-4PM	
4-5PM	
5-6PM	
6-7PM	
7-8PM	
8-9PM	
9-10PM	
10-11PM	
11PM-12AM	

> "NO MAN IS MORE UNHAPPY THAN HE WHO NEVER FACES ADVERSITY. FOR HE IS NOT PERMITTED TO PROVE HIMSELF."
> SENECA

DAY: DATE:

IMPORTANT STUFF (3/5)

GET SHIT DONE

	☐
	☐
	☐
	☐
	☐
	☐
	☐
	☐
	☐
	☐
	☐

DAILY REVIEW   SCORE: [ ]

5-6AM	
6-7AM	
7-8AM	
8-9AM	
9-10AM	
10-11AM	
11AM-12PM	
12-1PM	
1-2PM	
2-3PM	
3-4PM	
4-5PM	
5-6PM	
6-7PM	
7-8PM	
8-9PM	
9-10PM	
10-11PM	
11PM-12AM	

**"LEAD ME, FOLLOW ME,
OR GET THE HELL OUT OF MY WAY."
GEORGE S. PATTON**

WEEK 4

WEEKLY BRAINDUMP

RANK

WEEKLY BRAINDUMP

MY 3 BIG GOALS REMINDER: WHAT AM I FOCUSING ON THIS MONTH?

1

2

3

NOTES

DAY: DATE:

IMPORTANT STUFF (3/5)		5-6AM	

5-6AM	
6-7AM	
7-8AM	
8-9AM	
9-10AM	
10-11AM	
11AM-12PM	
12-1PM	
1-2PM	
2-3PM	
3-4PM	
4-5PM	
5-6PM	
6-7PM	
7-8PM	
8-9PM	
9-10PM	
10-11PM	
11PM-12AM	

IMPORTANT STUFF (3/5)

GET SHIT DONE

- ☐
- ☐
- ☐
- ☐
- ☐
- ☐
- ☐
- ☐
- ☐
- ☐
- ☐
- ☐

DAILY REVIEW   SCORE: [ ]

"I LEARNED THAT COURAGE WAS NOT THE ABSENCE OF FEAR, BUT THE TRIUMPH OVER IT. THE BRAVE MAN IS NOT HE WHO DOES NOT FEEL AFRAID, BUT HE WHO CONQUERS THAT FEAR."
NELSON MANDELA

NOTES

DAY: DATE:

IMPORTANT STUFF (3/5)		5-6AM	

IMPORTANT STUFF (3/5)

_____

_____

_____

_____

. . . .

GET SHIT DONE

_____ ☐

_____ ☐

_____ ☐

_____ ☐

_____ ☐

_____ ☐

_____ ☐

_____ ☐

_____ ☐

_____ ☐

_____ ☐

_____ ☐

DAILY REVIEW   SCORE: [   ]

_____

_____

_____

_____

Time	
5-6AM	
6-7AM	
7-8AM	
8-9AM	
9-10AM	
10-11AM	
11AM-12PM	
12-1PM	
1-2PM	
2-3PM	
3-4PM	
4-5PM	
5-6PM	
6-7PM	
7-8PM	
8-9PM	
9-10PM	
10-11PM	
11PM-12AM	

"WHAT THE ANCIENTS CALLED A CLEVER FIGHTER IS ONE WHO NOT ONLY WINS, BUT EXCELS IN WINNING WITH EASE."
SUN TZU

DAY: **DATE:**

IMPORTANT STUFF (3/5)

GET SHIT DONE

- [ ]
- [ ]
- [ ]
- [ ]
- [ ]
- [ ]
- [ ]
- [ ]
- [ ]
- [ ]
- [ ]

DAILY REVIEW **SCORE:**

5-6AM	
6-7AM	
7-8AM	
8-9AM	
9-10AM	
10-11AM	
11AM-12PM	
12-1PM	
1-2PM	
2-3PM	
3-4PM	
4-5PM	
5-6PM	
6-7PM	
7-8PM	
8-9PM	
9-10PM	
10-11PM	
11PM-12AM	

"ALL OF US DO NOT HAVE EQUAL TALENT, BUT ALL OF US SHOULD HAVE AN EQUAL OPPORTUNITY TO DEVELOP OUR TALENTS."
JOHN F. KENNEDY

DAY: DATE:

IMPORTANT STUFF (3/5)

5-6AM	
6-7AM	
7-8AM	
8-9AM	
9-10AM	
10-11AM	

GET SHIT DONE

☐	11AM-12PM	
☐	12-1PM	
☐	1-2PM	
☐	2-3PM	
☐	3-4PM	
☐	4-5PM	
☐	5-6PM	
☐	6-7PM	
☐	7-8PM	
☐	8-9PM	
☐	9-10PM	
☐	10-11PM	

DAILY REVIEW   SCORE: [ ]

11PM-12AM	

"I KNOW MY FATE. I AM NO MAN,
I AM DYNAMITE."
FRIEDRICH NIETZSCHE

DAY: DATE:

IMPORTANT STUFF (3/5)

5-6AM	
6-7AM	
7-8AM	
8-9AM	
9-10AM	
10-11AM	
11AM-12PM	

GET SHIT DONE

- [ ]
- [ ]
- [ ]
- [ ]
- [ ]
- [ ]
- [ ]
- [ ]
- [ ]
- [ ]
- [ ]

12-1PM	
1-2PM	
2-3PM	
3-4PM	
4-5PM	
5-6PM	
6-7PM	
7-8PM	
8-9PM	
9-10PM	
10-11PM	
11PM-12AM	

DAILY REVIEW   SCORE:

"THE SUPERIOR MAN IS HE WHO DEVELOPS, IN HARMONIOUS PROPORTIONS, HIS MORAL, INTELLECTUAL AND PHYSICAL NATURE. THIS SHOULD BE THE END AT WHICH MEN OF ALL CLASSES SHOULD AIM, AND IT IS THIS ONLY WHICH CONSTITUTES REAL GREATNESS." DOUGLAS JERROLD

DAY: DATE:

IMPORTANT STUFF (3/5)		5-6AM	

6-7AM	

7-8AM	

8-9AM	

9-10AM	

10-11AM	

GET SHIT DONE

	□	11AM-12PM	
	□	12-1PM	
	□	1-2PM	
	□	2-3PM	
	□	3-4PM	
	□	4-5PM	
	□	5-6PM	
	□	6-7PM	
	□	7-8PM	
	□	8-9PM	
	□	9-10PM	
	□	10-11PM	

DAILY REVIEW	SCORE:	11PM-12AM	

> "ONE MORE DANCE ALONG THE RAZOR'S EDGE
> FINISHED. ALMOST DEAD YESTERDAY,
> MAYBE DEAD TOMORROW, BUT ALIVE,
> GLORIOUSLY ALIVE, TODAY."
> ROBERT JORDAN

DAY: DATE:

IMPORTANT STUFF (3/5)

	5-6AM	

GET SHIT DONE

	☐

5-6AM	
6-7AM	
7-8AM	
8-9AM	
9-10AM	
10-11AM	
11AM-12PM	
12-1PM	
1-2PM	
2-3PM	
3-4PM	
4-5PM	
5-6PM	
6-7PM	
7-8PM	
8-9PM	
9-10PM	
10-11PM	
11PM-12AM	

DAILY REVIEW   SCORE: ☐

"MAKE BIG PLANS; AIM HIGH IN HOPE AND WORK,
REMEMBERING THAT A NOBLE, LOGICAL DIAGRAM
ONCE RECORDED WILL NOT DIE."
DANIEL BURNHAM

NOTES

MONTHLY BIG GOAL REVIEW

It's time to review your month. Rate your goals below, scoring from 1-10 (1=shit, 10=awesome) for IMPLEMENTATION (IMP) and RESULTS (RES) and then write any notes, both positive and negative, on the line to the right.

IMP   RES

1

A ☐ ☐ _____

B ☐ ☐ _____

C ☐ ☐ _____

2

A ☐ ☐ _____

B ☐ ☐ _____

C ☐ ☐ _____

3

A ☐ ☐ _____

B ☐ ☐ _____

C ☐ ☐ _____

TOTAL SCORE: IMPLEMENTATION ☐ **RESULTS:** ☐ **TOTAL:** ☐

WHAT HAS BEEN YOUR BIGGEST LESSON THIS MONTH AND HOW WILL YOU USE IT TO MAKE NEXT MONTH EVEN BETTER?

MONTHLY LIFE AUDIT

SCORE

BUSINESS	
BANK BALANCE	
NETWORK	
CAREER	
FRIENDSHIPS	
RELATIONSHIPS	
FITNESS	
REST AND RELAXATION	
TOTAL SCORE	

MONTHLY LIFE AUDIT REVIEW

NOTES

THE BIG 3: MONTH AHEAD GOAL SETTING

GOAL:

1

A:

B:

C:

GOAL:

2

A:

B:

C:

GOAL:

3

A:

B:

C:

MY 'GOT SHIT DONE' REWARD FOR SMASHING THIS MONTH

WEEK 5

IT'S F*CKING EASY TO BITCH ABOUT X OR Y, WHO ARE DOING Z. WHY NOT FOCUS ON BUILDING YOUR OWN TRIBE, YOUR OWN BRAND AND STOP CARING SO MUCH ABOUT WHAT OTHER PEOPLE ARE DOING.

#BeMoreDan

WEEKLY BRAINDUMP

RANK

MY 3 BIG GOALS REMINDER: WHAT AM I FOCUSING ON THIS MONTH?

1

2

3

DAY: DATE:

IMPORTANT STUFF (3/5)		5-6AM	
		6-7AM	
		7-8AM	
		8-9AM	
		9-10AM	
		10-11AM	
GET SHIT DONE		11AM-12PM	
	☐	12-1PM	
	☐	1-2PM	
	☐	2-3PM	
	☐	3-4PM	
	☐	4-5PM	
	☐	5-6PM	
	☐	6-7PM	
	☐	7-8PM	
	☐	8-9PM	
	☐	9-10PM	
	☐	10-11PM	
DAILY REVIEW	SCORE:	11PM-12AM	

"IF PLAN A FAILS, REMEMBER THERE ARE 25 MORE LETTERS IN THE ALPHABET."

NOTES

DAY: DATE:

IMPORTANT STUFF (3/5)		5-6AM	

	6-7AM
	7-8AM
	8-9AM
	9-10AM
	10-11AM

GET SHIT DONE

	☐	11AM-12PM
	☐	12-1PM
	☐	1-2PM
	☐	2-3PM
	☐	3-4PM
	☐	4-5PM
	☐	5-6PM
	☐	6-7PM
	☐	7-8PM
	☐	8-9PM
	☐	9-10PM
	☐	10-11PM

| DAILY REVIEW | SCORE: [ ] | 11PM-12AM |

"WE HAVE STRATEGIC PLAN, IT'S CALLED DOING THINGS."
HERB KELLEHER

NOTES

DAY:

DATE:

IMPORTANT STUFF (3/5)

GET SHIT DONE

- ☐
- ☐
- ☐
- ☐
- ☐
- ☐
- ☐
- ☐
- ☐
- ☐
- ☐
- ☐
- ☐
- ☐

DAILY REVIEW   SCORE:

5-6AM	
6-7AM	
7-8AM	
8-9AM	
9-10AM	
10-11AM	
11AM-12PM	
12-1PM	
1-2PM	
2-3PM	
3-4PM	
4-5PM	
5-6PM	
6-7PM	
7-8PM	
8-9PM	
9-10PM	
10-11PM	
11PM-12AM	

"PROCEED AS PLANNED."

DAY: DATE:

IMPORTANT STUFF (3/5)

GET SHIT DONE

☐
☐
☐
☐
☐
☐
☐
☐
☐
☐
☐
☐

DAILY REVIEW   SCORE:

5-6AM	
6-7AM	
7-8AM	
8-9AM	
9-10AM	
10-11AM	
11AM-12PM	
12-1PM	
1-2PM	
2-3PM	
3-4PM	
4-5PM	
5-6PM	
6-7PM	
7-8PM	
8-9PM	
9-10PM	
10-11PM	
11PM-12AM	

"MEASURE TWICE, CUT ONCE."

DAY: DATE:

IMPORTANT STUFF (3/5)

	5-6AM
	6-7AM
	7-8AM
	8-9AM
	9-10AM
	10-11AM

GET SHIT DONE

	☐	11AM-12PM
	☐	12-1PM
	☐	1-2PM
	☐	2-3PM
	☐	3-4PM
	☐	4-5PM
	☐	5-6PM
	☐	6-7PM
	☐	7-8PM
	☐	8-9PM
	☐	9-10PM
	☐	10-11PM

DAILY REVIEW   SCORE: [ ]

	11PM-12AM

**"REMEMBER THE SIX P'S:
PROPER PREPARATION PREVENTS
PISS POOR PERFORMANCE."**

DAY: DATE:

IMPORTANT STUFF (3/5)		5-6AM	

IMPORTANT STUFF (3/5)

GET SHIT DONE	
	☐
	☐
	☐
	☐
	☐
	☐
	☐
	☐
	☐
	☐
	☐

DAILY REVIEW	SCORE:

5-6AM	
6-7AM	
7-8AM	
8-9AM	
9-10AM	
10-11AM	
11AM-12PM	
12-1PM	
1-2PM	
2-3PM	
3-4PM	
4-5PM	
5-6PM	
6-7PM	
7-8PM	
8-9PM	
9-10PM	
10-11PM	
11PM-12AM	

"PLANS ARE OF LITTLE IMPORTANCE, BUT PLANNING IS ESSENTIAL."
WINSTON CHURCHILL

DAY: DATE:

IMPORTANT STUFF (3/5)

GET SHIT DONE

☐
☐
☐
☐
☐
☐
☐
☐
☐
☐
☐
☐

DAILY REVIEW   SCORE: ☐

5-6AM	
6-7AM	
7-8AM	
8-9AM	
9-10AM	
10-11AM	
11AM-12PM	
12-1PM	
1-2PM	
2-3PM	
3-4PM	
4-5PM	
5-6PM	
6-7PM	
7-8PM	
8-9PM	
9-10PM	
10-11PM	
11PM-12AM	

"GOOD FORTUNE IS WHAT HAPPENS WHEN OPPORTUNITY MEETS WITH PLANNING."
THOMAS EDISON

WEEK 6

WEEKLY BRAINDUMP

RAN

IT'S. OK. TO. ASK. FOR. HELP.

#BeMoreDan

WEEKLY BRAINDUMP

RANK

MY 3 BIG GOALS REMINDER: WHAT AM I FOCUSING ON THIS MONTH?

1

2

3

DAY: DATE:

IMPORTANT STUFF (3/5)

	5-6AM
	6-7AM
	7-8AM
	8-9AM
	9-10AM
	10-11AM

GET SHIT DONE

☐	11AM-12PM
☐	12-1PM
☐	1-2PM
☐	2-3PM
☐	3-4PM
☐	4-5PM
☐	5-6PM
☐	6-7PM
☐	7-8PM
☐	8-9PM
☐	9-10PM
☐	10-11PM

DAILY REVIEW   SCORE: ____

11PM-12AM

"THERE IS NO SUBSTITUTE FOR HARD WORK,
23 OR 24 HOURS A DAY. AND THERE IS NO
SUBSTITUTE FOR PATIENCE AND ACCEPTANCE."
CESAR CHAVEZ

NOTES

DAY: DATE:

IMPORTANT STUFF (3/5)

GET SHIT DONE

- [ ]
- [ ]
- [ ]
- [ ]
- [ ]
- [ ]
- [ ]
- [ ]
- [ ]
- [ ]
- [ ]

DAILY REVIEW   SCORE: [ ]

5-6AM	
6-7AM	
7-8AM	
8-9AM	
9-10AM	
10-11AM	
11AM-12PM	
12-1PM	
1-2PM	
2-3PM	
3-4PM	
4-5PM	
5-6PM	
6-7PM	
7-8PM	
8-9PM	
9-10PM	
10-11PM	
11PM-12AM	

"DON'T FIGHT THE PROBLEM, DECIDE IT."
GEORGE MARSHALL

NOTES

DAY: DATE:

IMPORTANT STUFF (3/5)

5-6AM	
6-7AM	
7-8AM	
8-9AM	
9-10AM	
10-11AM	
11AM-12PM	
12-1PM	
1-2PM	
2-3PM	
3-4PM	
4-5PM	
5-6PM	
6-7PM	
7-8PM	
8-9PM	
9-10PM	
10-11PM	
11PM-12AM	

GET SHIT DONE

☐
☐
☐
☐
☐
☐
☐
☐
☐
☐
☐

DAILY REVIEW   SCORE:

"NO MATTER HOW MANY TIMES I BREAK DOWN,
THERE IS ALWAYS A LITTLE PIECE OF ME SAYS
NO, YOU'RE NOT DONE YET GET BACK UP!"

DAY: DATE:

IMPORTANT STUFF (3/5)

GET SHIT DONE

☐
☐
☐
☐
☐
☐
☐
☐
☐
☐
☐
☐
☐
☐

DAILY REVIEW   SCORE: ☐

5-6AM	
6-7AM	
7-8AM	
8-9AM	
9-10AM	
10-11AM	
11AM-12PM	
12-1PM	
1-2PM	
2-3PM	
3-4PM	
4-5PM	
5-6PM	
6-7PM	
7-8PM	
8-9PM	
9-10PM	
10-11PM	
11PM-12AM	

"ALWAYS BE YOURSELF. EXPRESS YOURSELF. HAVE FAITH IN YOURSELF."
BRUCE LEE

NOTES

DAY: DATE:

IMPORTANT STUFF (3/5)

GET SHIT DONE	
	☐
	☐
	☐
	☐
	☐
	☐
	☐
	☐
	☐
	☐

DAILY REVIEW	SCORE:

5-6AM	
6-7AM	
7-8AM	
8-9AM	
9-10AM	
10-11AM	
11AM-12PM	
12-1PM	
1-2PM	
2-3PM	
3-4PM	
4-5PM	
5-6PM	
6-7PM	
7-8PM	
8-9PM	
9-10PM	
10-11PM	
11PM-12AM	

"THE OPINION OF 10,000 MEN IS OF
NO VALUE IF NONE OF THEM KNOW
ANYTHING ABOUT THE SUBJECT."
MARCUS AURELIUS

NOTES

DAY: DATE:

IMPORTANT STUFF (3/5)		5-6AM	

IMPORTANT STUFF (3/5)

GET SHIT DONE	
	☐
	☐
	☐
	☐
	☐
	☐
	☐
	☐
	☐
	☐

DAILY REVIEW	**SCORE:**

5-6AM	
6-7AM	
7-8AM	
8-9AM	
9-10AM	
10-11AM	
11AM-12PM	
12-1PM	
1-2PM	
2-3PM	
3-4PM	
4-5PM	
5-6PM	
6-7PM	
7-8PM	
8-9PM	
9-10PM	
10-11PM	
11PM-12AM	

"I'M NOT THE BEST. I JUST BELIEVE I CAN DO THINGS THAT PEOPLE THINK ARE IMPOSSIBLE."
ANDERSON SILVA

DAY: DATE:

IMPORTANT STUFF (3/5)

GET SHIT DONE

☐
☐
☐
☐
☐
☐
☐
☐
☐
☐
☐
☐

DAILY REVIEW   SCORE: [   ]

5-6AM	
6-7AM	
7-8AM	
8-9AM	
9-10AM	
10-11AM	
11AM-12PM	
12-1PM	
1-2PM	
2-3PM	
3-4PM	
4-5PM	
5-6PM	
6-7PM	
7-8PM	
8-9PM	
9-10PM	
10-11PM	
11PM-12AM	

**"WHAT'S THE USE OF RUNNING
IF YOU ARE NOT ON THE RIGHT ROAD?"
GERMAN PROVERB**

WEEK 7

WEEKLY BRAINDUMP

**WE ALL HAVE TO START SOMEWHERE – THE KEY THING?
IT'S F*CKING STARTING!**

#BeMoreDan

WEEKLY BRAINDUMP

MY 3 BIG GOALS REMINDER: WHAT AM I FOCUSING ON THIS MONTH?

1

2

3

NOTES

DAY: DATE:

IMPORTANT STUFF (3/5)

5-6AM	
6-7AM	
7-8AM	
8-9AM	
9-10AM	
10-11AM	
11AM-12PM	
12-1PM	
1-2PM	
2-3PM	
3-4PM	
4-5PM	
5-6PM	
6-7PM	
7-8PM	
8-9PM	
9-10PM	
10-11PM	
11PM-12AM	

GET SHIT DONE

- ☐
- ☐
- ☐
- ☐
- ☐
- ☐
- ☐
- ☐
- ☐
- ☐
- ☐
- ☐
- ☐

DAILY REVIEW   SCORE: [   ]

> "IF THE RESULTS DON'T SCREAM:
> 'DO THIS AGAIN!' TRY SOMETHING NEW."
> TONY ROBBINS

DAY: DATE:

IMPORTANT STUFF (3/5)		5-6AM	

IMPORTANT STUFF (3/5)

5-6AM	
6-7AM	
7-8AM	
8-9AM	
9-10AM	
10-11AM	
11AM-12PM	
12-1PM	
1-2PM	
2-3PM	
3-4PM	
4-5PM	
5-6PM	
6-7PM	
7-8PM	
8-9PM	
9-10PM	
10-11PM	
11PM-12AM	

GET SHIT DONE

☐
☐
☐
☐
☐
☐
☐
☐
☐
☐
☐
☐
☐

DAILY REVIEW   **SCORE:** [ ]

NOTES

DAY: DATE:

IMPORTANT STUFF (3/5)

GET SHIT DONE

- ☐
- ☐
- ☐
- ☐
- ☐
- ☐
- ☐
- ☐
- ☐
- ☐
- ☐
- ☐

DAILY REVIEW   SCORE: [ ]

5-6AM	
6-7AM	
7-8AM	
8-9AM	
9-10AM	
10-11AM	
11AM-12PM	
12-1PM	
1-2PM	
2-3PM	
3-4PM	
4-5PM	
5-6PM	
6-7PM	
7-8PM	
8-9PM	
9-10PM	
10-11PM	
11PM-12AM	

> "HE WHO BELIEVES IS STRONG; HE WHO DOUBTS IS WEAK. STRONG CONVICTIONS PRECEDE GREAT ACTIONS."
> LOUISA MAY ALCOTT

DAY: DATE:

IMPORTANT STUFF (3/5)

5-6AM	
6-7AM	
7-8AM	
8-9AM	
9-10AM	
10-11AM	
11AM-12PM	
12-1PM	
1-2PM	
2-3PM	
3-4PM	
4-5PM	
5-6PM	
6-7PM	
7-8PM	
8-9PM	
9-10PM	
10-11PM	
11PM-12AM	

GET SHIT DONE

☐
☐
☐
☐
☐
☐
☐
☐
☐
☐
☐
☐

DAILY REVIEW   SCORE: ☐

"PERMANENCE, PERSEVERANCE AND PERSISTENCE IN SPITE OF ALL OBSTACLES, DISCOURAGEMENTS, AND IMPOSSIBILITIES: IT IS THIS, THAT IN ALL THINGS DISTINGUISHES THE STRONG SOUL FROM THE WEAK."
THOMAS CARLYLE

NOTES

DAY: DATE:

IMPORTANT STUFF (3/5)

GET SHIT DONE

- [ ]
- [ ]
- [ ]
- [ ]
- [ ]
- [ ]
- [ ]
- [ ]
- [ ]
- [ ]
- [ ]

DAILY REVIEW   SCORE:

5-6AM	
6-7AM	
7-8AM	
8-9AM	
9-10AM	
10-11AM	
11AM-12PM	
12-1PM	
1-2PM	
2-3PM	
3-4PM	
4-5PM	
5-6PM	
6-7PM	
7-8PM	
8-9PM	
9-10PM	
10-11PM	
11PM-12AM	

"YOU CANNOT DREAM YOURSELF INTO A
CHARACTER; YOU MUST HAMMER
AND FORGE YOURSELF ONE."
JAMES A. FROUDE

147

NOTES

DAY:

DATE:

IMPORTANT STUFF (3/5)		5-6AM	
		6-7AM	
		7-8AM	
		8-9AM	
		9-10AM	
		10-11AM	
GET SHIT DONE		11AM-12PM	
	☐	12-1PM	
	☐	1-2PM	
	☐	2-3PM	
	☐	3-4PM	
	☐	4-5PM	
	☐	5-6PM	
	☐	6-7PM	
	☐	7-8PM	
	☐	8-9PM	
	☐	9-10PM	
	☐	10-11PM	
DAILY REVIEW SCORE:		11PM-12AM	

DAY: DATE:

IMPORTANT STUFF (3/5)		5-6AM	

5-6AM	
6-7AM	
7-8AM	
8-9AM	
9-10AM	
10-11AM	
11AM-12PM	
12-1PM	
1-2PM	
2-3PM	
3-4PM	
4-5PM	
5-6PM	
6-7PM	
7-8PM	
8-9PM	
9-10PM	
10-11PM	
11PM-12AM	

IMPORTANT STUFF (3/5)

GET SHIT DONE

☐
☐
☐
☐
☐
☐
☐
☐
☐
☐
☐
☐

DAILY REVIEW   SCORE: ☐

"THE HAPPINESS OF YOUR LIFE DEPENDS UPON
THE QUALITY OF YOUR THOUGHTS."
MARCUS AURELIUS

WEEK 8

WEEKLY BRAINDUMP

**NO ONE IS BETTER THAN YOU.
THEY ARE SIMPLY FURTHER ALONG
OR HAVE INVESTED MORE TIME THAN YOU.**

#BeMoreDan

WEEKLY BRAINDUMP

RANK

MY 3 BIG GOALS REMINDER: WHAT AM I FOCUSING ON THIS MONTH?
1
2
3

DAY:

DATE:

IMPORTANT STUFF (3/5)

GET SHIT DONE

	☐
	☐
	☐
	☐
	☐
	☐
	☐
	☐
	☐
	☐
	☐
	☐

DAILY REVIEW   SCORE: [   ]

5-6AM	
6-7AM	
7-8AM	
8-9AM	
9-10AM	
10-11AM	
11AM-12PM	
12-1PM	
1-2PM	
2-3PM	
3-4PM	
4-5PM	
5-6PM	
6-7PM	
7-8PM	
8-9PM	
9-10PM	
10-11PM	
11PM-12AM	

"SHALLOW MEN BELIEVE IN LUCK. STRONG MEN BELIEVE IN CAUSE AND EFFECT."
RALPH WALDO EMERSON

NOTES

DAY: DATE:

IMPORTANT STUFF (3/5)		5-6AM	
		6-7AM	
		7-8AM	
		8-9AM	
		9-10AM	
		10-11AM	
GET SHIT DONE		11AM-12PM	
	☐	12-1PM	
	☐	1-2PM	
	☐	2-3PM	
	☐	3-4PM	
	☐	4-5PM	
	☐	5-6PM	
	☐	6-7PM	
	☐	7-8PM	
	☐	8-9PM	
	☐	9-10PM	
	☐	10-11PM	
DAILY REVIEW	SCORE: ☐	11PM-12AM	

"WHEN YOU LOOSE ALL YOUR EXCUSES, YOU WILL START FINDING YOUR RESULTS."

NOTES

DAY: DATE:

IMPORTANT STUFF (3/5)

5-6AM	
6-7AM	
7-8AM	
8-9AM	
9-10AM	
10-11AM	
11AM-12PM	
12-1PM	
1-2PM	
2-3PM	
3-4PM	
4-5PM	
5-6PM	
6-7PM	
7-8PM	
8-9PM	
9-10PM	
10-11PM	
11PM-12AM	

GET SHIT DONE

- [ ]
- [ ]
- [ ]
- [ ]
- [ ]
- [ ]
- [ ]
- [ ]
- [ ]
- [ ]
- [ ]

DAILY REVIEW   SCORE:

"IN THE ANIMAL KINGDOM, THE RULE IS,
EAT OR BE EATEN; IN THE HUMAN KINGDOM,
DEFINE OR BE DEFINED."
THOMAS SZASZ

NOTES

DAY: DATE:

IMPORTANT STUFF (3/5)		5-6AM	

IMPORTANT STUFF (3/5)

GET SHIT DONE	
	☐
	☐
	☐
	☐
	☐
	☐
	☐
	☐
	☐
	☐
	☐

DAILY REVIEW	SCORE:

5-6AM	
6-7AM	
7-8AM	
8-9AM	
9-10AM	
10-11AM	
11AM-12PM	
12-1PM	
1-2PM	
2-3PM	
3-4PM	
4-5PM	
5-6PM	
6-7PM	
7-8PM	
8-9PM	
9-10PM	
10-11PM	
11PM-12AM	

"SCAR TISSUE IS STRONGER THAN REGULAR TISSUE. REALISE THE STRENGTH, MOVE ON."
HENRY ROLLINS

NOTES

DAY: DATE:

IMPORTANT STUFF (3/5)

5-6AM	
6-7AM	
7-8AM	
8-9AM	
9-10AM	
10-11AM	
11AM-12PM	
12-1PM	
1-2PM	
2-3PM	
3-4PM	
4-5PM	
5-6PM	
6-7PM	
7-8PM	
8-9PM	
9-10PM	
10-11PM	
11PM-12AM	

GET SHIT DONE

- [ ]
- [ ]
- [ ]
- [ ]
- [ ]
- [ ]
- [ ]
- [ ]
- [ ]
- [ ]
- [ ]
- [ ]
- [ ]

DAILY REVIEW   SCORE:

"KNOWLEDGE IS POWER BUT ENTHUSIASM PULLS THE SWITCH."

DAY:

DATE:

IMPORTANT STUFF (3/5)

GET SHIT DONE

	☐
	☐
	☐
	☐
	☐
	☐
	☐
	☐
	☐
	☐
	☐
	☐

DAILY REVIEW   SCORE: [ ]

5-6AM	
6-7AM	
7-8AM	
8-9AM	
9-10AM	
10-11AM	
11AM-12PM	
12-1PM	
1-2PM	
2-3PM	
3-4PM	
4-5PM	
5-6PM	
6-7PM	
7-8PM	
8-9PM	
9-10PM	
10-11PM	
11PM-12AM	

"A BRAVE MAN, A REAL FIGHTER, IS NOT MEASURED BY HOW MANY TIMES HE FALLS, BUT HOW MANY TIMES HE STANDS UP."
RICKSON GRACIE

NOTES

DAY: DATE:

IMPORTANT STUFF (3/5)

GET SHIT DONE

	☐
	☐
	☐
	☐
	☐
	☐
	☐
	☐
	☐
	☐
	☐

DAILY REVIEW   SCORE: [ ]

5-6AM	
6-7AM	
7-8AM	
8-9AM	
9-10AM	
10-11AM	
11AM-12PM	
12-1PM	
1-2PM	
2-3PM	
3-4PM	
4-5PM	
5-6PM	
6-7PM	
7-8PM	
8-9PM	
9-10PM	
10-11PM	
11PM-12AM	

"THERE IS NOTHING IMPOSSIBLE TO HIM WHO WILL TRY."
ALEXANDER THE GREAT

169

MONTHLY BIG GOAL REVIEW

It's time to review your month. Rate your goals below, scoring from 1-10 (1=shit, 10=awesome) for IMPLEMENTATION (IMP) and RESULTS (RES) and then write any notes, both positive and negative, on the line to the right.

IMP   RES

1

A ☐ ☐ _____

B ☐ ☐ _____

C ☐ ☐ _____

2

A ☐ ☐ _____

B ☐ ☐ _____

C ☐ ☐ _____

3

A ☐ ☐ _____

B ☐ ☐ _____

C ☐ ☐ _____

TOTAL SCORE: IMPLEMENTATION ☐ **RESULTS:** ☐ **TOTAL:** ☐

WHAT HAS BEEN YOUR BIGGEST LESSON THIS MONTH AND HOW WILL YOU USE IT TO MAKE NEXT MONTH EVEN BETTER?

MONTHLY LIFE AUDIT

SCORE

BUSINESS	
BANK BALANCE	
NETWORK	
CAREER	
FRIENDSHIPS	
RELATIONSHIPS	
FITNESS	
REST AND RELAXATION	
TOTAL SCORE	

MONTHLY LIFE AUDIT REVIEW

THE BIG 3: MONTH AHEAD GOAL SETTING

GOAL:

1

A:

B:

C:

GOAL:

2

A:

B:

C:

GOAL:

3

A:

B:

C:

MY 'GOT SHIT DONE' REWARD FOR SMASHING THIS MONTH

WEEK 9

WEEKLY BRAINDUMP

RANK

'DOES IT SERVE YOU?'
RUN EVERYTHING THROUGH THAT FILTER.

#BeMoreDan

WEEKLY BRAINDUMP

RANK

MY 3 BIG GOALS REMINDER: WHAT AM I FOCUSING ON THIS MONTH?

1	
2	
3	

DAY: DATE:

IMPORTANT STUFF (3/5)

	5-6AM	
	6-7AM	
	7-8AM	
	8-9AM	
	9-10AM	
	10-11AM	

GET SHIT DONE

		11AM-12PM	
	☐	12-1PM	
	☐	1-2PM	
	☐	2-3PM	
	☐	3-4PM	
	☐	4-5PM	
	☐	5-6PM	
	☐	6-7PM	
	☐	7-8PM	
	☐	8-9PM	
	☐	9-10PM	
	☐	10-11PM	

DAILY REVIEW   SCORE: [   ]

11PM-12AM

> "I CAME. I SAW. I CONQUERED."
> **JULIUS CAESAR**

DAY: DATE:

IMPORTANT STUFF (3/5)

5-6AM	
6-7AM	
7-8AM	
8-9AM	
9-10AM	
10-11AM	

GET SHIT DONE

11AM-12PM	
12-1PM	
1-2PM	
2-3PM	
3-4PM	
4-5PM	
5-6PM	
6-7PM	
7-8PM	
8-9PM	
9-10PM	
10-11PM	

DAILY REVIEW   SCORE:

11PM-12AM	

> "CLEAR OUT THE PAST, LAYOUT THE PRESENT AND PREPARE FOR A MUCH BETTER AND BRIGHTER FUTURE."
> OMOAKHUANA ANTHONIA

DAY: DATE:

IMPORTANT STUFF (3/5)

....

GET SHIT DONE

☐
☐
☐
☐
☐
☐
☐
☐
☐
☐
☐
☐

DAILY REVIEW   SCORE: [____]

5-6AM	
6-7AM	
7-8AM	
8-9AM	
9-10AM	
10-11AM	
11AM-12PM	
12-1PM	
1-2PM	
2-3PM	
3-4PM	
4-5PM	
5-6PM	
6-7PM	
7-8PM	
8-9PM	
9-10PM	
10-11PM	
11PM-12AM	

"TOMORROW IS NOT JUST A DAY THAT CAN'T BE SEEN, IT IS A DAY THAT CAN ONLY BE SEEN BY THE DECISIONS WE MAKE TODAY."
AULIQ ICE

DAY: DATE:

IMPORTANT STUFF (3/5)			

	5-6AM	
	6-7AM	
	7-8AM	
	8-9AM	
	9-10AM	
	10-11AM	
GET SHIT DONE	11AM-12PM	
☐	12-1PM	
☐	1-2PM	
☐	2-3PM	
☐	3-4PM	
☐	4-5PM	
☐	5-6PM	
☐	6-7PM	
☐	7-8PM	
☐	8-9PM	
☐	9-10PM	
☐	10-11PM	
DAILY REVIEW SCORE: ☐	11PM-12AM	

> "PLANS ARE ONLY GOOD INTENTIONS
> UNLESS THEY IMMEDIATELY
> DEGENERATE INTO HARD WORK."
> PETER DRUCKER

DAY: **DATE:**

IMPORTANT STUFF (3/5)

GET SHIT DONE

- [ ]
- [ ]
- [ ]
- [ ]
- [ ]
- [ ]
- [ ]
- [ ]
- [ ]
- [ ]
- [ ]

DAILY REVIEW

SCORE:

5-6AM	
6-7AM	
7-8AM	
8-9AM	
9-10AM	
10-11AM	
11AM-12PM	
12-1PM	
1-2PM	
2-3PM	
3-4PM	
4-5PM	
5-6PM	
6-7PM	
7-8PM	
8-9PM	
9-10PM	
10-11PM	
11PM-12AM	

"BITE OFF MORE THAN YOU CAN CHEW, THEN CHEW IT. PLAN MORE THAN YOU CAN DO, THEN DO IT."

NOTES

DAY: DATE:

IMPORTANT STUFF (3/5)			5-6AM	

IMPORTANT STUFF (3/5)

GET SHIT DONE

	5-6AM	
	6-7AM	
	7-8AM	
	8-9AM	
	9-10AM	
	10-11AM	
	11AM-12PM	
☐	12-1PM	
☐	1-2PM	
☐	2-3PM	
☐	3-4PM	
☐	4-5PM	
☐	5-6PM	
☐	6-7PM	
☐	7-8PM	
☐	8-9PM	
☐	9-10PM	
☐	10-11PM	

DAILY REVIEW   **SCORE:** ☐

11PM-12AM	

**"MAKE NO LITTLE PLANS; THEY HAVE NO MAGIC
TO STIR MEN'S BLOOD... MAKE BIG PLANS,
AIM HIGH IN HOPE AND WORK."**
DANIEL H. BURNHAM

NOTES

DAY: DATE:

IMPORTANT STUFF (3/5)

GET SHIT DONE

	☐
	☐
	☐
	☐
	☐
	☐
	☐
	☐
	☐
	☐
	☐
	☐

DAILY REVIEW   SCORE: [ ]

Time	
5-6AM	
6-7AM	
7-8AM	
8-9AM	
9-10AM	
10-11AM	
11AM-12PM	
12-1PM	
1-2PM	
2-3PM	
3-4PM	
4-5PM	
5-6PM	
6-7PM	
7-8PM	
8-9PM	
9-10PM	
10-11PM	
11PM-12AM	

"ORGANISE, DON'T AGONISE."
NANCY PELOSI

WEEK 10

WEEKLY BRAINDUMP

RANK

THE COLD TRUTHS, ALTHOUGH PAINFUL, ARE OFTEN
THE ONES THAT DO YOU THE BEST IN THE LONG RUN.

#BeMoreDan

WEEKLY BRAINDUMP

	RANK

MY 3 BIG GOALS REMINDER: WHAT AM I FOCUSING ON THIS MONTH?
1
2
3

NOTES

DAY: DATE:

IMPORTANT STUFF (3/5)		5-6AM	

IMPORTANT STUFF (3/5)

GET SHIT DONE

	☐
	☐
	☐
	☐
	☐
	☐
	☐
	☐
	☐
	☐
	☐

DAILY REVIEW	SCORE:

5-6AM	
6-7AM	
7-8AM	
8-9AM	
9-10AM	
10-11AM	
11AM-12PM	
12-1PM	
1-2PM	
2-3PM	
3-4PM	
4-5PM	
5-6PM	
6-7PM	
7-8PM	
8-9PM	
9-10PM	
10-11PM	
11PM-12AM	

> "CREATE A DEFINITE PLAN FOR CARRYING OUT
> YOUR DESIRE AND BEGIN AT ONCE,
> WHETHER YOU ARE READY OR NOT,
> TO PUT THIS PLAN INTO ACTION."
> NAPOLEON HILL

NOTES

DAY: DATE:

IMPORTANT STUFF (3/5)

GET SHIT DONE	
	☐
	☐
	☐
	☐
	☐
	☐
	☐
	☐
	☐
	☐

DAILY REVIEW	SCORE:

5-6AM	
6-7AM	
7-8AM	
8-9AM	
9-10AM	
10-11AM	
11AM-12PM	
12-1PM	
1-2PM	
2-3PM	
3-4PM	
4-5PM	
5-6PM	
6-7PM	
7-8PM	
8-9PM	
9-10PM	
10-11PM	
11PM-12AM	

"JUST BECAUSE SOMETHING DOESN'T
DO WHAT YOU PLANNED IT TO DO
DOESN'T MEAN IT'S USELESS."
THOMAS A. EDISON

NOTES

DAY: DATE:

IMPORTANT STUFF (3/5)		5-6AM	
		6-7AM	
		7-8AM	
		8-9AM	
		9-10AM	
		10-11AM	
GET SHIT DONE		11AM-12PM	
	☐	12-1PM	
	☐	1-2PM	
	☐	2-3PM	
	☐	3-4PM	
	☐	4-5PM	
	☐	5-6PM	
	☐	6-7PM	
	☐	7-8PM	
	☐	8-9PM	
	☐	9-10PM	
	☐	10-11PM	
DAILY REVIEW	SCORE:	11PM-12AM	

> "DON'T SIT AROUND WAITING FOR RESULTS.
> IF YOU WANT TO START SOMETHING
> PUT IT OUT THERE TODAY."
> **THOMAS EDISON**

NOTES

DAY:

DATE:

IMPORTANT STUFF (3/5)

GET SHIT DONE

	☐
	☐
	☐
	☐
	☐
	☐
	☐
	☐
	☐
	☐
	☐
	☐

DAILY REVIEW   SCORE: [ ]

5-6AM	
6-7AM	
7-8AM	
8-9AM	
9-10AM	
10-11AM	
11AM-12PM	
12-1PM	
1-2PM	
2-3PM	
3-4PM	
4-5PM	
5-6PM	
6-7PM	
7-8PM	
8-9PM	
9-10PM	
10-11PM	
11PM-12AM	

"WE MUST DARE TO BE GREAT; AND WE MUST
REALIZE THAT GREATNESS IS THE FRUIT OF TOIL
AND SACRIFICE AND HIGH COURAGE."
THODORE ROOSEVELT

NOTES

DAY: DATE:

IMPORTANT STUFF (3/5)

5-6AM	
6-7AM	
7-8AM	
8-9AM	
9-10AM	
10-11AM	

GET SHIT DONE

11AM-12PM	
12-1PM	
1-2PM	
2-3PM	
3-4PM	
4-5PM	
5-6PM	
6-7PM	
7-8PM	
8-9PM	
9-10PM	
10-11PM	

DAILY REVIEW   SCORE:

11PM-12AM

> "KNOWING IS NOT ENOUGH. WE MUST APPLY.
> WILLING IN NOT ENOUGH. WE MUST DO."
> BRUCE LEE

NOTES

DAY: DATE:

IMPORTANT STUFF (3/5)

5-6AM	
6-7AM	
7-8AM	
8-9AM	
9-10AM	
10-11AM	
11AM-12PM	

GET SHIT DONE

	☐	12-1PM	
	☐	1-2PM	
	☐	2-3PM	
	☐	3-4PM	
	☐	4-5PM	
	☐	5-6PM	
	☐	6-7PM	
	☐	7-8PM	
	☐	8-9PM	
	☐	9-10PM	
	☐	10-11PM	

DAILY REVIEW   SCORE: ☐

| 11PM-12AM | |

"A TARGET SHOULD GO WITH EVERY GOAL. A TARGET IS THE VALUE THAT DEFINES SUCCESS."
MICHAEL PORTER

DAY: **DATE:**

IMPORTANT STUFF (3/5)

| |
| |
| |
| |
| |

GET SHIT DONE

	☐
	☐
	☐
	☐
	☐
	☐
	☐
	☐
	☐
	☐
	☐
	☐

DAILY REVIEW   SCORE: [   ]

| |
| |
| |

5-6AM	
6-7AM	
7-8AM	
8-9AM	
9-10AM	
10-11AM	
11AM-12PM	
12-1PM	
1-2PM	
2-3PM	
3-4PM	
4-5PM	
5-6PM	
6-7PM	
7-8PM	
8-9PM	
9-10PM	
10-11PM	
11PM-12AM	

"YOU CANNOT SUCCEED IN A VACUUM; THERE NEEDS TO BE SUBSTANCE AND RESISTANCE OR YOUR WORLD IS NO MORE THAN A DREAM."
BYRON PULSIFER

WEEK 11

WEEKLY BRAINDUMP

RANK

REMEMBER: FIT YOUR OWN OXYGEN MASK FIRST!

#BeMoreDan

WEEKLY BRAINDUMP

RANK

MY 3 BIG GOALS REMINDER: WHAT AM I FOCUSING ON THIS MONTH?

1

2

3

DAY: DATE:

IMPORTANT STUFF (3/5)			5-6AM	

IMPORTANT STUFF (3/5)

GET SHIT DONE	
	☐
	☐
	☐
	☐
	☐
	☐
	☐
	☐
	☐
	☐
	☐
	☐

DAILY REVIEW	**SCORE:**

5-6AM	
6-7AM	
7-8AM	
8-9AM	
9-10AM	
10-11AM	
11AM-12PM	
12-1PM	
1-2PM	
2-3PM	
3-4PM	
4-5PM	
5-6PM	
6-7PM	
7-8PM	
8-9PM	
9-10PM	
10-11PM	
11PM-12AM	

**"THERE IS NO SUCH THING AS FAILURE.
THERE ARE ONLY RESULTS."
TONY ROBBINS**

NOTES

DAY: DATE:

IMPORTANT STUFF (3/5)

GET SHIT DONE

	☐
	☐
	☐
	☐
	☐
	☐
	☐
	☐
	☐
	☐
	☐

DAILY REVIEW   SCORE:

5-6AM	
6-7AM	
7-8AM	
8-9AM	
9-10AM	
10-11AM	
11AM-12PM	
12-1PM	
1-2PM	
2-3PM	
3-4PM	
4-5PM	
5-6PM	
6-7PM	
7-8PM	
8-9PM	
9-10PM	
10-11PM	
11PM-12AM	

"SOMETIMES THE BEST SOLUTION IS SIMPLIFICATION."
BOBBY BRAGAN

DAY: DATE:

IMPORTANT STUFF (3/5)		5-6AM	
		6-7AM	
		7-8AM	
		8-9AM	
		9-10AM	
		10-11AM	
GET SHIT DONE		11AM-12PM	
	☐	12-1PM	
	☐	1-2PM	
	☐	2-3PM	
	☐	3-4PM	
	☐	4-5PM	
	☐	5-6PM	
	☐	6-7PM	
	☐	7-8PM	
	☐	8-9PM	
	☐	9-10PM	
	☐	10-11PM	
DAILY REVIEW SCORE:		11PM-12AM	

"HOPE IS NOT A STRATEGY."
COLIN POWELL

DAY: DATE:

IMPORTANT STUFF (3/5)

GET SHIT DONE

- [ ]
- [ ]
- [ ]
- [ ]
- [ ]
- [ ]
- [ ]
- [ ]
- [ ]
- [ ]
- [ ]

DAILY REVIEW   SCORE:

5-6AM	
6-7AM	
7-8AM	
8-9AM	
9-10AM	
10-11AM	
11AM-12PM	
12-1PM	
1-2PM	
2-3PM	
3-4PM	
4-5PM	
5-6PM	
6-7PM	
7-8PM	
8-9PM	
9-10PM	
10-11PM	
11PM-12AM	

"IF PEOPLE KNEW HOW HARD I WORKED TO ACHIEVE MY MASTERY, IT WOULDN'T SEEM SO WONDERFUL AFTER ALL."
MICHELANGELO

DAY: DATE:

IMPORTANT STUFF (3/5)		5-6AM	

IMPORTANT STUFF (3/5)

GET SHIT DONE	
	☐
	☐
	☐
	☐
	☐
	☐
	☐
	☐
	☐
	☐

DAILY REVIEW	SCORE:

5-6AM	
6-7AM	
7-8AM	
8-9AM	
9-10AM	
10-11AM	
11AM-12PM	
12-1PM	
1-2PM	
2-3PM	
3-4PM	
4-5PM	
5-6PM	
6-7PM	
7-8PM	
8-9PM	
9-10PM	
10-11PM	
11PM-12AM	

"THINK CRAZILY, EVEN IF OTHERS LAUGH AT YOU.
ACT BRAVELY, EVEN IF YOU ARE ALL ALONE."
DILIP BATHIJA

NOTES

DAY: DATE:

IMPORTANT STUFF (3/5)		5-6AM	

IMPORTANT STUFF (3/5)

GET SHIT DONE

	☐
	☐
	☐
	☐
	☐
	☐
	☐
	☐
	☐
	☐
	☐

DAILY REVIEW   SCORE: [ ]

5-6AM	
6-7AM	
7-8AM	
8-9AM	
9-10AM	
10-11AM	
11AM-12PM	
12-1PM	
1-2PM	
2-3PM	
3-4PM	
4-5PM	
5-6PM	
6-7PM	
7-8PM	
8-9PM	
9-10PM	
10-11PM	
11PM-12AM	

"DON'T BE AFRAID THAT YOU DON'T HAVE WHAT IT TAKES TO GET SHIT DONE. JUST START DOING IT!"
TONY STARK

DAY: DATE:

IMPORTANT STUFF (3/5)

GET SHIT DONE

☐
☐
☐
☐
☐
☐
☐
☐
☐
☐
☐

DAILY REVIEW   SCORE: [ ]

5-6AM	
6-7AM	
7-8AM	
8-9AM	
9-10AM	
10-11AM	
11AM-12PM	
12-1PM	
1-2PM	
2-3PM	
3-4PM	
4-5PM	
5-6PM	
6-7PM	
7-8PM	
8-9PM	
9-10PM	
10-11PM	
11PM-12AM	

"TO WIN TAKES A COMPLETE COMMITMENT OF MIND AND BODY. WHEN YOU CAN'T MAKE THAT COMMITMENT, THEY DON'T CALL YOU A CHAMPION ANYMORE"
ROCKY MARCIANO

WEEK 12

WEEKLY BRAINDUMP

RANK

**EFFORT, SHOWING UP, COMMITMENT, PASSION,
DRIVE AND SACRIFICE (FOR A PERIOD)
ARE ALL KEY PLAYERS IN MAKING IT ONLINE.**

#BeMoreDan

WEEKLY BRAINDUMP

MY 3 BIG GOALS REMINDER: WHAT AM I FOCUSING ON THIS MONTH?

1	
2	
3	

DAY: **DATE:**

IMPORTANT STUFF (3/5)

5-6AM	
6-7AM	
7-8AM	
8-9AM	
9-10AM	
10-11AM	
11AM-12PM	

GET SHIT DONE

	☐	12-1PM	
	☐	1-2PM	
	☐	2-3PM	
	☐	3-4PM	
	☐	4-5PM	
	☐	5-6PM	
	☐	6-7PM	
	☐	7-8PM	
	☐	8-9PM	
	☐	9-10PM	
	☐	10-11PM	

DAILY REVIEW   SCORE: ☐

11PM-12AM	

"IT'S THE REPETITION OF AFFIRMATIONS THAT LEADS TO BELIEF. AND ONCE THAT BELIEF BECOMES A DEEP CONVICTION, THINGS BEGIN TO HAPPEN."
MUHAMMAD ALI

NOTES

DAY: **DATE:**

IMPORTANT STUFF (3/5)

GET SHIT DONE

	☐
	☐
	☐
	☐
	☐
	☐
	☐
	☐
	☐
	☐
	☐

DAILY REVIEW   SCORE:

5-6AM	
6-7AM	
7-8AM	
8-9AM	
9-10AM	
10-11AM	
11AM-12PM	
12-1PM	
1-2PM	
2-3PM	
3-4PM	
4-5PM	
5-6PM	
6-7PM	
7-8PM	
8-9PM	
9-10PM	
10-11PM	
11PM-12AM	

"IF YOU DO WHAT YOU HAVE ALWAYS DONE, YOU WILL GET WHAT YOU HAVE ALWAYS GOT"
MARK TWAIN

DAY: **DATE:**

IMPORTANT STUFF (3/5)	

GET SHIT DONE	
	☐
	☐
	☐
	☐
	☐
	☐
	☐
	☐
	☐
	☐
	☐
	☐

DAILY REVIEW	**SCORE:**	

5-6AM	
6-7AM	
7-8AM	
8-9AM	
9-10AM	
10-11AM	
11AM-12PM	
12-1PM	
1-2PM	
2-3PM	
3-4PM	
4-5PM	
5-6PM	
6-7PM	
7-8PM	
8-9PM	
9-10PM	
10-11PM	
11PM-12AM	

"GREAT INNOVATION ONLY HAPPENS WHEN PEOPLE AREN'T AFRAID TO DO THINGS DIFFERENTLY."
GEORGE CANTOR

NOTES

DAY: DATE:

IMPORTANT STUFF (3/5)		5-6AM	

IMPORTANT STUFF (3/5)

GET SHIT DONE	
	☐
	☐
	☐
	☐
	☐
	☐
	☐
	☐
	☐
	☐
	☐

DAILY REVIEW	SCORE:

5-6AM	
6-7AM	
7-8AM	
8-9AM	
9-10AM	
10-11AM	
11AM-12PM	
12-1PM	
1-2PM	
2-3PM	
3-4PM	
4-5PM	
5-6PM	
6-7PM	
7-8PM	
8-9PM	
9-10PM	
10-11PM	
11PM-12AM	

> "IF YOU ALWAYS PUT LIMITS ON EVERYTHING YOU DO, PHYSICAL OR ANYTHING ELSE, IT WILL SPREAD INTO YOUR WORK AND INTO YOUR LIFE. THERE ARE NO LIMITS. THERE ARE ONLY PLATEAUS, AND YOU MUST NOT STAY THERE, YOU MUST GO BEYOND THEM." BRUCE LEE

DAY: DATE:

IMPORTANT STUFF (3/5)		5-6AM	
		6-7AM	
		7-8AM	
		8-9AM	
		9-10AM	
		10-11AM	
GET SHIT DONE		11AM-12PM	
	☐	12-1PM	
	☐	1-2PM	
	☐	2-3PM	
	☐	3-4PM	
	☐	4-5PM	
	☐	5-6PM	
	☐	6-7PM	
	☐	7-8PM	
	☐	8-9PM	
	☐	9-10PM	
	☐	10-11PM	
DAILY REVIEW SCORE:		11PM-12AM	

> "THOSE WHO SPEAK OF PROGRESSION BUT ARE AFRAID OF CHANGE ARE SELF-REPRESSED AND THEREFORE UNABLE TO REACH ANY FURTHER THAN THEIR EYES CAN ALREADY SEE."
> CRISS JAMI

DAY: DATE:

IMPORTANT STUFF (3/5)

GET SHIT DONE	
	☐
	☐
	☐
	☐
	☐
	☐
	☐
	☐
	☐
	☐

DAILY REVIEW	SCORE:

5-6AM	
6-7AM	
7-8AM	
8-9AM	
9-10AM	
10-11AM	
11AM-12PM	
12-1PM	
1-2PM	
2-3PM	
3-4PM	
4-5PM	
5-6PM	
6-7PM	
7-8PM	
8-9PM	
9-10PM	
10-11PM	
11PM-12AM	

"THE QUESTION IN LIFE IS NOT WHETHER YOU GET KNOCKED DOWN. YOU WILL. THE QUESTION IS, ARE YOU READY TO GET BACKUP... AND FIGHT FOR WHAT YOU BELIEVE IN?"
DAN QUAYLE

DAY: DATE:

IMPORTANT STUFF (3/5)		5-6AM	
		6-7AM	
		7-8AM	
		8-9AM	
		9-10AM	
		10-11AM	
GET SHIT DONE		11AM-12PM	
	☐	12-1PM	
	☐	1-2PM	
	☐	2-3PM	
	☐	3-4PM	
	☐	4-5PM	
	☐	5-6PM	
	☐	6-7PM	
	☐	7-8PM	
	☐	8-9PM	
	☐	9-10PM	
	☐	10-11PM	
DAILY REVIEW SCORE:		11PM-12AM	

"COURAGE IS CONTAGIOUS.
WHEN A BRAVE MAN TAKES A STAND,
THE SPINES OF OTHERS ARE OFTEN STIFFENED."
BILLY GRAHAM

NOTES

MONTHLY BIG GOAL REVIEW

It's time to review your month. Rate your goals below, scoring from 1-10 (1=shit, 10=awesome) for IMPLEMENTATION (IMP) and RESULTS (RES) and then write any notes, both positive and negative, on the line to the right.

IMP   RES

1

A ☐ ☐ _____

B ☐ ☐ _____

C ☐ ☐ _____

2

A ☐ ☐ _____

B ☐ ☐ _____

C ☐ ☐ _____

3

A ☐ ☐ _____

B ☐ ☐ _____

C ☐ ☐ _____

TOTAL SCORE: IMPLEMENTATION ☐ **RESULTS:** ☐ **TOTAL:** ☐

WHAT HAS BEEN YOUR BIGGEST LESSON THIS MONTH AND HOW WILL YOU USE IT TO MAKE NEXT MONTH EVEN BETTER?

MONTHLY LIFE AUDIT

	SCORE
BUSINESS	
BANK BALANCE	
NETWORK	
CAREER	
FRIENDSHIPS	
RELATIONSHIPS	
FITNESS	
REST AND RELAXATION	
TOTAL SCORE	

MONTHLY LIFE AUDIT REVIEW

12 WEEK
REVIEW

LIFE REVIEW

What does your life look like now? Is it what you planned back on page 15?
If yes, how are you going to celebrate? If no, what could you do better next time?
Write your thoughts below...

MY 12 WEEKS

WINS	LOSSES

KEEP IN TOUCH

Want some more accountability?

Need a kick up the arse or an arm round the shoulder as you work your way through your goals?

Join me in **Coffee With Dan**. #Simples.

At first, I really didn't know why my group has become as large as it has. It started off as a bit of fun to keep me accountable. Now there are thousands of talented, motivated people in the group, who publically hold themselves accountable.

If you are a member, FFS don't just lurk! Be active. Ask questions. Give answers where you can. It's so much easier to live outside your comfort zone with others by your side. Don't grind along alone reinventing the wheel, instead learn from someone else in the group who's done it already.

This bunch of nutcases can also help you achieve the big goals you're setting for yourself over the next 90 days. #UseIt #BeMoreDan

You can find out more at

WWW.COFFEEWITHDAN.COM

and if it seems like it's for you, you're welcome to join.

WANT EVEN MORE DAN?

I practice what I preach. If you want more help and insights from me,
join my mailing list.

I share more hints and tips and also let you know about free online training me and
my team of experts offer **Coffee With Dan** members.

Relax, it's not just a lame, one-way "newsletter" style mailing, it has actionable stuff.
I do monitor my emails.

Well, to get on my email list I'm going to offer you something of value FIRST.
I wrote and ebook called '**30 Things I learned From The Most Ridiculous
Year Of My Life....So Far!**', where I talk your though all the highs and lows of
becoming an entrepreneur.

You can grab it at **www.coffeewithdan.com/30things**

Once you do? You will automatically be added to my subscriber list, or if you want
to go all 'old school' you can email me on dan@coffeewithdan.com

I actually do give a shit about the people who invest in me and my products,
so I hope to hear from you soon.

TTFN

Dan

ABOUT THE AUTHOR

Hi, I'm Dan.

I get shit done, and I'm rather surprised how successful I am.

I like to work hard and do dumb things on social media purely for my own entertainment. I also like to write a lot of things and launch businesses, because why the fuck not!?

I'm not the sharpest tool in the shed, but it seems to work.

Cheers!

Dan